GEO

FRIEND
OF ACPL

P9-DYP-185

3/06

Lexile: _____

AR/BL: _____3.7_____

AR Points: ____0.5____

A Note to Parents and Teachers

Kids can imagine, kids can laugh and kids can learn to read with this exciting new series of first readers. Each book in the Kids Can Read series has been especially written, illustrated and designed for beginning readers. Humorous, easy-to-read stories, appealing characters and engaging illustrations make for books that kids will want to read over and over again.

To make selecting a book easy for kids, parents and teachers, the Kids Can Read series offers three levels based on different reading abilities:

Level 1: Kids Can Start to Read

Short stories, simple sentences, easy vocabulary, lots of repetition and visual clues for kids just beginning to read.

Level 2: Kids Can Read with Help

Longer stories, varied sentences, increased vocabulary, some repetition and visual clues for kids who have some reading skills, but may need a little help.

Level 3: Kids Can Read Alone

Longer, more complex stories and sentences, more challenging vocabulary, language play, minimal repetition and visual clues for kids who are reading by themselves.

With the Kids Can Read series, kids can enter a new and exciting world of reading!

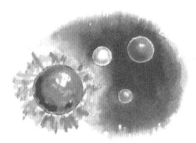

DISCOVER THE STARS

Written by Cynthia Pratt Nicolson
Illustrated by Bill Slavin

Kids Can Press

I am grateful to Stan Shadick of the University of Saskatchewan, Grant Hill of the Dominion Astrophysical Observatory and Colin Scarfe of the University of Victoria for sharing their expert knowledge, and infectious sense of wonder, about the stars. — C.P.N.

★ Kids Can Read ® Kids Can Read is a registered trademark of Kids Can Press Ltd.

Text © 1998 Cynthia Pratt Nicolson
Illustrations © 1998 Bill Slavin
Revised edition © 2006

All rights reserved. No part of this publication may be reproduced, stored in a retrieval system or transmitted, in any form or by any means, without the prior written permission of Kids Can Press Ltd. or, in case of photocopying or other reprographic copying, a license from The Canadian Copyright Licensing Agency (Access Copyright). For an Access Copyright license, visit www.accesscopyright.ca or call toll free to 1-800-893-5777.

Kids Can Press acknowledges the financial support of the Government of Ontario, through the Ontario Media Development Corporation's Ontario Book Initiative; the Ontario Arts Council; the Canada Council for the Arts; and the Government of Canada, through the BPIDP, for our publishing activity.

Published in Canada by
Kids Can Press Ltd.
29 Birch Avenue
Toronto, ON M4V 1E2

Published in the U.S. by
Kids Can Press Ltd.
2250 Military Road
Tonawanda, NY 14150

www.kidscanpress.com

Adapted by David MacDonald and Cynthia Pratt Nicolson from the book *The Stars*.

Edited by Jennifer Stokes
Designed by Sherill Chapman
Educational consultant: Maureen Skinner Weiner, United Synagogue Day School, Willowdale, Ontario

Photo Credits
All photos used courtesy of NASA except page 12 © Roger Ressmeyer/CORBIS and page 13 © Roger Ressmeyer/CORBIS.

Printed and bound in China

The hardcover edition of this book is smyth sewn casebound.
The paperback edition of this book is limp sewn with a drawn-on cover.

CM 06 0 9 8 7 6 5 4 3 2 1
CM PA 06 0 9 8 7 6 5 4 3 2 1

Library and Archives Canada Cataloguing in Publication

Nicolson, Cynthia Pratt
    Discover the stars / written by Cynthia Pratt Nicolson ; illustrated by Bill Slavin.

(Kids can read)
Adaptation of The Stars, first published 1998 in the Starting with space series.

Age level: 6–8.

ISBN-13: 978-1-55337-898-3 (bound).   ISBN-10: 1-55337-898-9 (bound).
ISBN-13: 978-1-55337-899-0 (pbk.)   ISBN-10: 1-55337-899-7 (pbk.)

1. Stars — Juvenile literature. I. Slavin, Bill II. Nicolson, Cynthia Pratt. Stars. III. Title. IV. Series: Kids Can read (Toronto, Ont.)

QB801.7.N52 2006   j523.8   C2005-902111-X

Kids Can Press is a **ᒪ©ᖳᒍS** ™ Entertainment company

CONTENTS

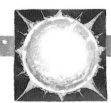

ALL ABOUT STARS

Look up at the sky on a dark, clear night. What do you see? Stars!

If you live in a city, you may not find many stars in the sky. The lights of a city make stars hard to see. But if you are far away from city lights, you can see thousands of stars!

Stars twinkle like tiny diamonds in the sky.

What is a star?

A star is a fiery ball in space. Even though stars are huge, they look tiny. Why? Because they are so far away!

A star is not like our planet, Earth. On Earth we have land and water. There is no land or water on a star.

Is the Sun a star?

Yes, the Sun is a star. It seems so big and bright because it is much closer to us than any other star. The glowing Sun gives us light and makes heat that warms the Earth.

This photo shows the Sun shining on Earth.

How many stars are there?

There are more stars in space than you could ever count. If you spent your whole life counting stars, you wouldn't be able to count them all!

The stars we see in the night sky are just some of the stars in space. There are lots of other stars that are too far away for us to see.

What color are the stars?

All the stars in the sky look white, but only a few actually are white. Cooler stars are a red or orange color. Hotter stars are light blue. Medium-hot stars, like our Sun, are yellow.

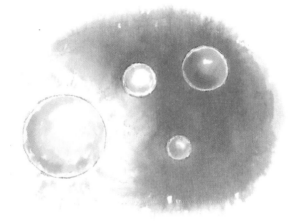

Are all stars far apart from each other?

No. Scientists have discovered that many stars come in pairs. Sometimes, two stars are so close together that they look like just one star.

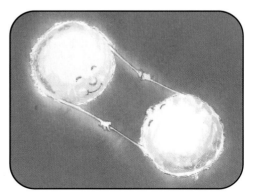

Are all stars the same size?

Stars come in many different sizes. Some stars are smaller than Earth. Some are bigger.

Our Sun is much bigger than Earth. The Sun is so big that a million Earths could fit inside it. And our Sun is just a medium-sized star! Many stars are much larger than our Sun.

What is the biggest star we can see from Earth?

The biggest star you can see in the sky is called Betelgeuse (bet-el-jooze). Betelgeuse is huge — it is 700 times bigger than the Sun.

This image of Betelgeuse was taken by the Hubble Space Telescope.

How far away are the stars?

The Sun is the closest star to Earth, but it's still very far away. If you flew in a jet plane from the Sun, it would take you 18 years to reach Earth.

Other stars are even farther away from Earth. The light from some stars takes hundreds or even thousands of years to get to Earth.

What is a shooting star?

Sometimes you can see a dot of light moving quickly across the night sky. Some people call these moving lights shooting stars. But they really aren't stars at all.

What looks like shooting stars are really tiny pieces of dust that fly through space. When the tiny pieces get close to Earth, they burn up and leave streaks of light across the sky. Scientists call these moving lights "meteors."

3 1833 04636 206 4

LOOKING AT STARS

Why can't we see stars during the day?

Stars are always there in the sky. We can't see them during the day because the Sun's light makes the sky too bright.

Imagine that a star is like a flashlight. If you shine a flashlight in a bright room, you can't see the beam of light it makes. But in a dark room, you can easily see the beam of light. That is why we can see stars only when it's dark out.

What is an astronomer?

An astronomer is a scientist who studies the stars. Can you see the word *astron* in "astronomer"? *Astron* means "star" in Greek.

How do scientists look at stars?

Scientists can use telescopes to look at stars. A telescope makes things that are far away look like they're much closer.

This telescope is at Chicago's Yerkes Observatory.

What is an observatory?

An observatory is a building with a huge telescope for looking out into space. With a very large telescope, astronomers can see stars far out in space that can't be seen with a small telescope.

A telescope in an observatory is too big and heavy for a person to move. An observatory has a motor to move the telescope. The motor points the telescope at different parts of the sky.

This is part of the Kitt Peak National Observatory in Arizona.

What is the Hubble Space Telescope?

The Hubble Space Telescope is a very large telescope that was sent into space. This telescope helps us to see things that we can't see with telescopes on Earth. The Hubble Space Telescope takes photos in space and sends them back to Earth.

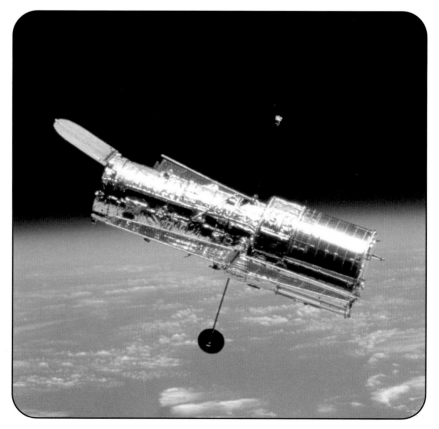

This is the Hubble Space Telescope.

Why did astronauts have to fix the Hubble Space Telescope?

When the Hubble Space Telescope started to send photos back from space, scientists were very disappointed. The pictures were blurry!

Astronauts went into space to fix the telescope. Now it sends back photos that are bright and clear.

Astronauts work to fix the Hubble Space Telescope.

Here are some amazing pictures the Hubble Space Telescope has taken of stars far out in space:

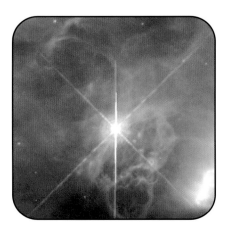

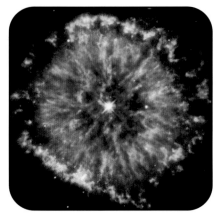

CONSTELLATIONS

What is a constellation?

A night sky full of stars looks like a giant connect-the-dots puzzle. If you could draw lines between some of the stars, you could make many different shapes.

When ancient people looked up at the stars, they saw shapes that reminded them of objects, animals and people in stories. Today, we call these star shapes constellations.

What shapes do you see in this starry sky?

Long ago, people told stories about the great hunter Orion. They named a constellation after him.

The picture at left shows Orion holding a club and a shield. The white dots inside the picture show the stars that make up the constellation called Orion.

The picture at right shows what Orion looks like in the night sky. Can you see the shape that makes up his body? Can you see Orion's belt?

What is the Southern Cross?

The Southern Cross is a constellation of four bright stars that make a shape like a cross.

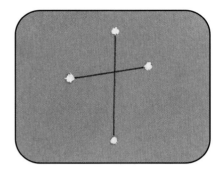

Are you wondering why this constellation is called the Southern Cross? It's because you can only see it if you are closer to the South Pole than you are to the North Pole.

Australia and New Zealand are two countries that are close to the South Pole. The flags for these countries show the Southern Cross.

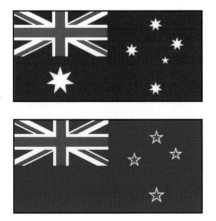

Australia's flag

New Zealand's flag

What is the Big Dipper?

The Big Dipper is made up of seven bright stars. These stars make a shape that looks like a pot with a long handle. This kind of pot was used as a dipper to take water from a pail. That's how the Big Dipper got its name.

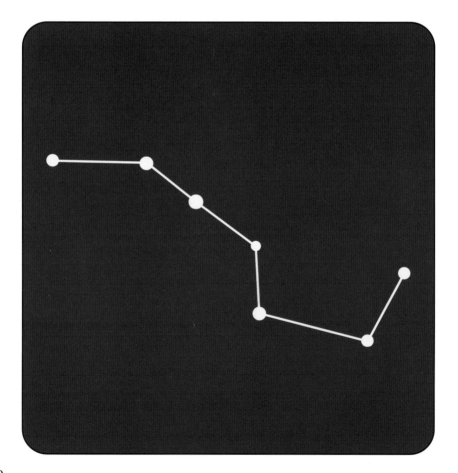

The Big Dipper is part
of a large constellation
called the Great Bear.
Can you see the
shape of a bear in
the constellation below?
Can you see the Big Dipper?

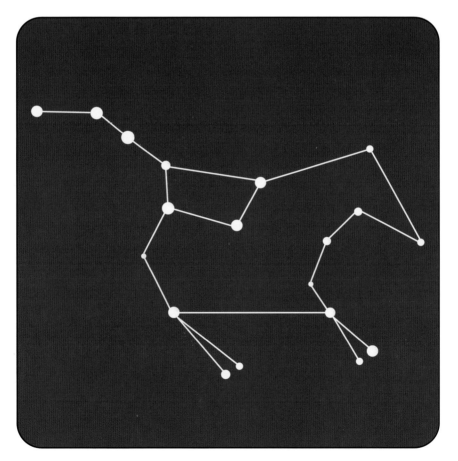

What is the North Star?

The North Star isn't a constellation, but it's a very important star. This star shows which direction is north.

Long ago, sailors used the North Star to make sure their ships were going in the right direction.

North Star

What are some other constellations?

There are 88 different constellations. Here are some more:

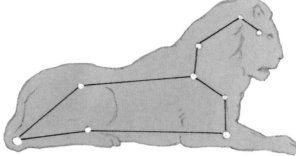

People call this constellation the Lion. The stars make a shape like a lion taking a rest.

This constellation is called the Bull. Can you see the stars that make up the bull's horns?

This constellation made people think of a pair of twins, so it's called the Twins.

The constellation below is called the Swan. These stars reminded people of a swan with its wings stretched wide.

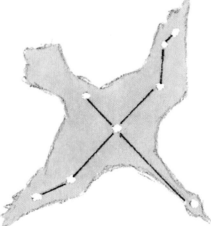

This constellation is called the Eagle. Can you see the stars that make the eagle's wings?

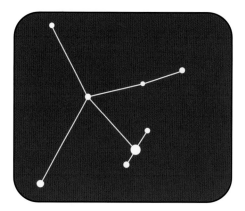

Can you guess what animal this constellation looks like?

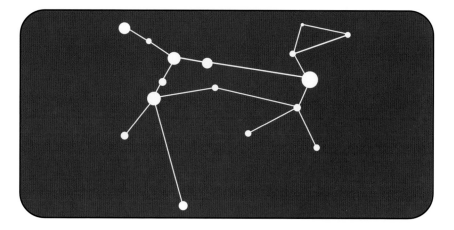

If you guessed a dog, you're right! This constellation is called the Great Dog.

Do constellations change?

If you could watch constellations for thousands of years, you would notice small changes in their shapes. Look at the pictures below. Can you see how the shape of the Big Dipper changes over time?

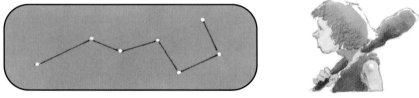 

This is what the Big Dipper looked like thousands of years ago.

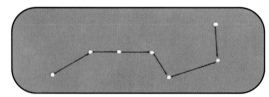 

This is what the Big Dipper looks like today.

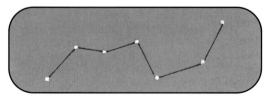

This is what the Big Dipper will look like thousands of years from now.

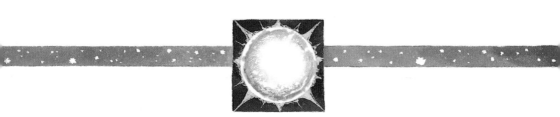

THE LIFE OF STARS

How do stars begin?

Imagine something that looks like a huge, swirling cloud in space. As the cloud swirls around, it gets smaller. As it gets smaller, it gets hotter and hotter. Finally, it gets so hot that it starts to burn. A star is born!

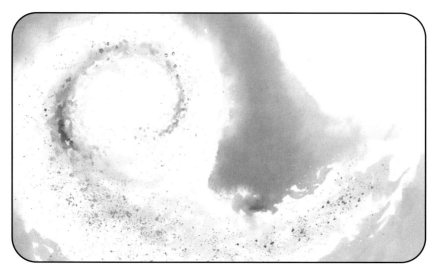

This picture gives you an idea of what a swirling cloud in space looks like. This swirling cloud will become a burning star.

How do stars grow old?

Over a very long time, stars begin to burn out. When this happens, they get bigger and become a reddish color. After that, the stars shrink to a much smaller size and become white.

These small white stars are called white dwarf stars. White dwarf stars are usually about the size of Earth.

The yellow stars in this photo are young stars. The stars with a more reddish color are older stars.

What is a supernova?

Sometimes giant stars explode at the end of their life. This explosion is called a supernova. A supernova is very bright!

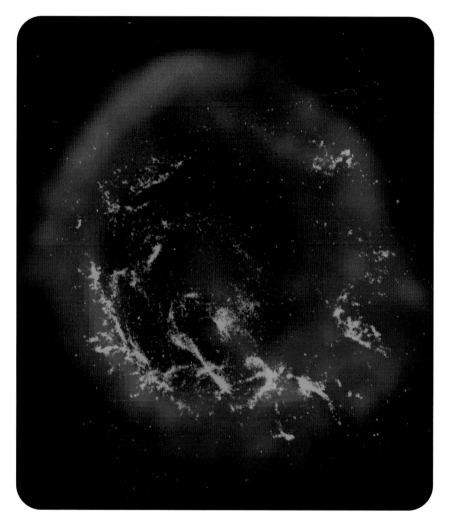

This is an amazing photo of an exploding star — a supernova!

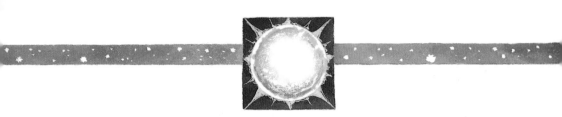

GALAXIES

What is a galaxy?

A galaxy is a huge group of stars. You can think of a galaxy as a city of stars.

Galaxies come in different shapes and sizes. Some galaxies look like blurry blobs. Other galaxies have clear shapes, like a hot dog or a pinwheel.

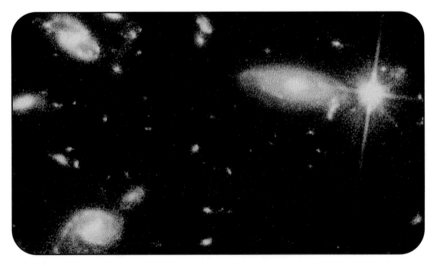

The Hubble Space Telescope took this picture, which shows several hundred galaxies.

What is the Milky Way?

The Milky Way is the name of the galaxy we live in. It has a shape like a pinwheel. The whole galaxy spins in space. Earth is near the outside edge of the Milky Way.

There are many, many stars in the Milky Way. The Sun is just one of those stars.

Earth is here

Do you look at the stars?

You don't have to be an astronomer to look at the stars. Just go outside on a clear night. Spread out a blanket, lie back and watch the show! Can you find the Big Dipper or Orion's belt? What about the Lion?

Use your imagination to find other patterns in the sky. You can even name your own constellations. For a better view, use a pair of binoculars. You'll be amazed at what you see!